The United States

North Carolina

Paul Joseph
ABDO & Daughters

visit us at
www.abdopub.com

Published by Abdo & Daughters, 4940 Viking Drive, Suite 622, Edina, Minnesota 55435. Copyright © 1998 by Abdo Consulting Group, Inc., Pentagon Tower, P.O. Box 36036, Minneapolis, Minnesota 55435 USA. International copyrights reserved in all countries. No part of this book may be reproduced in any form without written permission from the publisher.

Printed in the United States.

Cover and Interior Photo credits: Peter Arnold, Inc., SuperStock, Archive, Corbis-Bettmann

Edited by Lori Kinstad Pupeza
Contributing editor Brooke Henderson
Special thanks to our Checkerboard Kids—Aisha Baker, Priscilla Cáceres, Teddy Borth

All statistics taken from the 1990 census; The Rand McNally Discovery Atlas of The United States.

Library of Congress Cataloging-in-Publication Data

Joseph, Paul, 1970-
    North Carolina / Paul Joseph.
    p.   cm. -- (United States)
    Includes index.
    Summary: Includes information about the history, geography, and people of the Tarheel State.
    ISBN 1-56239-869-5
    1. North Carolina--Juvenile literature. [1. North Carolina.] I. Title. II. Series: United States (Series)
F254.3.J67   1998
975.6--dc21   97-18663
                                                                                                     CIP
                                                                                                     AC

Contents

Welcome to North Carolina 4

Fast Facts About North Carolina 6

Nature's Treasures 8

Beginnings 10

Happenings 12

North Carolina's People.................................. 18

Splendid Cities 20

North Carolina's Land 22

North Carolina at Play 24

North Carolina at Work 26

Fun Facts 28

Glossary 30

Internet Sites 31

Index 32

Welcome to North Carolina

The wonderful state of North Carolina is known as the Tar Heel State. People have come up with different reasons as to why it is the Tar Heel State. The most common reason was that when the British crossed the Tar River they found tar on their heels. Another story told was that Confederate soldiers threatened to put tar on the boots of cowardly soldiers so they would "stick better in the next fight." No matter what the reason, the nickname has stuck.

North Carolina is a wide and short state. From top to bottom its greatest distance is only 188 miles (302 km). From side to side it is 499 miles (803 km), the widest of any state east of the Mississippi River.

The beautiful land and wonderful climate of North Carolina attracts many people to the state. The land supports small farms as well as grazing areas for beef and dairy **cattle**. Two-thirds of North Carolina is forested. This makes for a scenic state as well as a huge lumbering **industry**. Because the state **borders** on the Atlantic Ocean, fishing industries are also important.

North Carolina is home to many interesting historic sites. The first English settlement was tried in the state. Also many battlefields of the **American Revolution** and the **Civil War** are located here. Near Kitty Hawk is where the Wright Brothers first flew an airplane.

North Carolina has beautiful forests and rivers.

Fast Facts

NORTH CAROLINA
Capital
Raleigh (207,951 people)
Area
48,843 square miles
(126,503 sq km)
Population
6,657,630 people
Rank: 10th
Statehood
November 21, 1789
(12th state admitted)
Principal rivers
Roanoke River, Neuse River, Cape Fear River
Highest point
Mount Mitchell;
6,684 feet (2,037 m)
Largest city
Charlotte (395,934 people)
Motto
Esse quam videri (To be rather than to seem)
Song
"The Old North State"
Famous People
Virginia Dare, Billy Graham, Andrew Johnson, Dolley Madison, James K. Polk, Wilbur and Orville Wright

North Carolina is one of the original 13 colonies

State Flag

Cardinal

Dogwood

Long leaf Pine

About North Carolina
The Tar Heel State

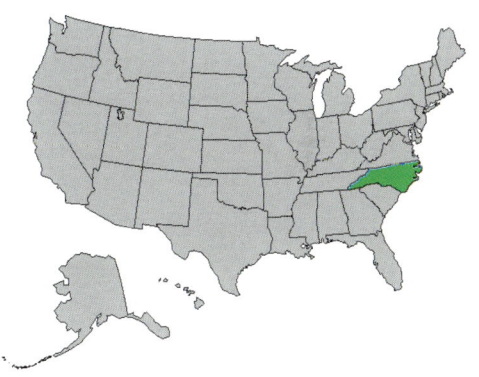

Borders: west (Tennessee), north (Virginia), east (Atlantic Ocean), south (Georgia, South Carolina)

Nature's Treasures

North Carolina has a great mixture of treasures in its state. There are breathtaking mountains, rich farmland, sandy beaches on the ocean, wonderful forests, and warm weather.

Many say the climate in North Carolina is its best treasure. The weather is usually very warm, with cool breezes off the Atlantic Ocean. In the west the high mountains protect the state from cold winds.

North Carolina has many farms. Tobacco, corn, cotton, and peanuts are North Carolina's major **crops**. Because most of the state is covered in forests, North Carolina has beautiful state parks.

When it comes to water, North Carolina has a lot of different types. There is the Atlantic Ocean with wonderful beaches. People can swim and fish in the lakes and rivers. And some of the swamp land has been turned into scenic state parks.

Tourists come by the thousands to the Tar Heel state for its treasures. There are not a lot of states that have as many treasures as North Carolina.

A lot of tobacco is grown in North Carolina.

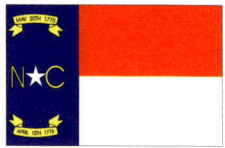

Beginnings

Before the arrival of Europeans, **Native Americans** lived in the area now called North Carolina. The most powerful Native Americans were the Cherokee and the Tuscarora. In the 1700s, the Tuscarora moved to New York. In the 1830s, the Cherokee were forced to move to Oklahoma in the tragic journey known as the Trail of Tears.

In 1584, Sir Walter Raleigh sent over English **explorers**. The next year Raleigh sent over a group that settled on Roanoke Island. Conflicts with the Native Americans and little food soon caused them to return to England.

In 1663, the Carolina region was doing very well. However, people were fighting over ownership. Finally in 1712, North Carolina and South Carolina became separate regions.

North Carolina fought for its independence from the English. Many battles took place and many soldiers were killed. Finally, on November 21, 1789, North Carolina became the 12th state.

In 1861, North Carolina left the Union to join other southern states to start their own country, called the Confederacy. Again many battles took place—this time between the North and the South. After the North defeated the South in the **Civil War**, North Carolina joined the union. The state was readmitted to the United States on July 20, 1868.

Native Americans building canoes in North Carolina.

Happenings • Happenings • Happenings • Happenings • Happenings • Happeni

B.C. to 1629

First People and Explorers

 Many millions of year ago North Carolina was covered in ice.

 Later, **Native Americans** lived in the area now called North Carolina.

 1584: Queen Elizabeth of England grants Sir Walter Raleigh the right to colonize America. He explores Roanoke Island.

 1629: King Charles I of England grants part of North Carolina to Sir Robert Heath. He names it "Carolina" after the king.

Happenings • Happenings • Happenings • Happenings • Happenings • Happenings

North Carolina
B.C. to 1629

Happenings • Happenings • Happenings • Happenings • Happenings • Happenings

1700s

Schools to Statehood

1705: The first school opened in Pasquotank County.

1712: Carolina divided into two provinces.

1789: North Carolina becomes the 12th state on November 21.

openings • Happenings • Happenings • Happenings • Happenings • Happenings

North Carolina
1700s

Happenings • Happenings • Happenings • Happenings • Happenings • Happeni

1829 to Now

Presidents, Flyers, and Sports Star

1829: Andrew Jackson, a Carolina native, is elected the seventh president of the United States.

1845: James K. Polk of Mecklenburg County becomes 11th president of the United States.

1865: Andrew Johnson of Raleigh becomes the 17th president of the United States.

1903: The Wright Brothers make the first airplane flight near Kitty Hawk, North Carolina.

1997: North Carolina native, Michael Jordan, leads the Chicago Bulls to their fifth NBA Championship.

Happenings • Happenings • Happenings • Happenings • Happenings • Happenings

North Carolina
1829 to Now

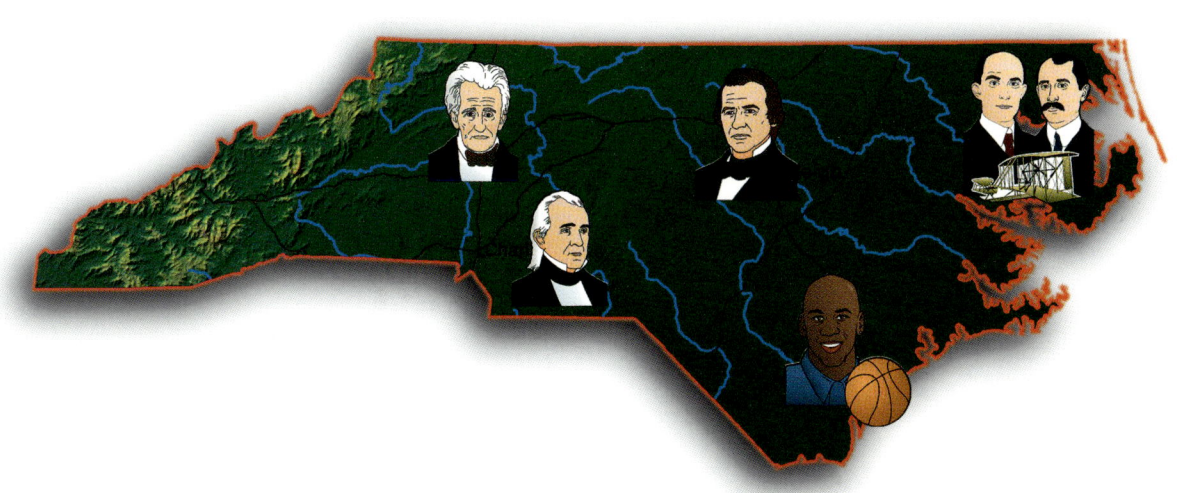

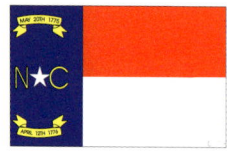

North Carolina's People

There are about 6.7 million people in North Carolina. The first known people to live in North Carolina were **Native Americans**.

North Carolina has also had many famous people come from its state. Three presidents of the United States were born in North Carolina. Andrew Jackson, born in 1767, was the seventh president. However, it is disputed as to whether he was born in North or South Carolina. James K. Polk was the 11th president. He was born in 1795, in Mecklenburg county. And Andrew Johnson was born in 1808, in Raleigh, and was the 17th president.

David Brinkley, a famous television journalist, was born in 1920, in Wilmington. Also from Wilmington is the world's most popular athlete—Michael Jordan. In 1963, he was born in New York, but a few years later he and his family moved to North Carolina. He is the star basketball player for the Chicago Bulls. He has led his team to five NBA Championships, an NCAA title in college for the University of North Carolina, and two gold medals for the United States Olympic team. To this day, Jordan still calls himself "a country boy from North Carolina."

Other famous people include movie star Ava Gardner, race car legend Richard Petty, and country singer Randy Travis.

David Brinkley

Michael Jordan

James K. Polk

Splendid Cities

North Carolina has many splendid cities. It also has many small towns and villages of less than 2,500 people. Around half of the **population** is in **rural** areas.

The largest city in the state is Charlotte, with almost 400,000 people. Charlotte is located in the south-central part of the state. Charlotte is a wonderful city with many exciting things to do. Lots of fans watch the Charlotte Hornets play basketball.

The capital of Raleigh is the second largest city with just over 200,000 people. Four colleges are in this fun city. They are North Carolina State University, Shaw University, St. Augustine's College, and Meredith College.

The historic city of Greensboro forms a tri-city with Winston-Salem and High Point. All three cities are known for their museums, shops, colleges, and tobacco **production**.

Other splendid cities include, Durham, the home of Duke University. Asheville, located near mountains, is known for being a winter and summer **resort**. And Chapel Hill is home of the University of North Carolina Tar Heels.

A rural scene near Linville, North Carolina.

North Carolina's Land

North Carolina has a lot of diverse land. From high mountains, to thick forests, to rich farmland, to rivers and lakes, to sandy beaches on the ocean, the Tar Heel State has it all. The land is divided into three parts.

The Mountain Region covers the western part of the state. This area has the beautiful Great Smoky Mountains and the Blue Ridge. People come from all over to see these mountain ranges.

Most of the Mountain Region is covered with forests—even to the top of most mountains. The highest point in the state is here. Mount Mitchell is 6,684 feet (2,037 m) tall. From its peak, seven states can be seen.

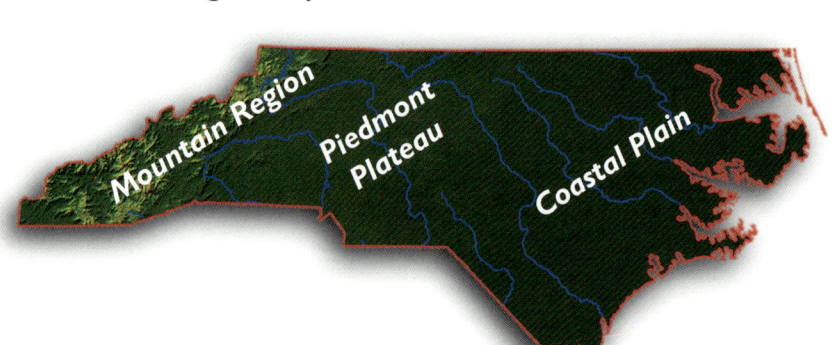

The Piedmont Region is in the central part of the state. It begins at the base of the Blue Ridge and extends eastward. It changes from hills to rolling country. The land has forests, rivers, and farm land.

The Coastal Plain is in the east and is the state's largest region. Most of its soil is rich, level, and sandy. The region is filled with forests, farms, and rivers.

Great Smoky Mountains, North Carolina.

North Carolina at Play

Because of the warm weather, people can enjoy the outdoors all year long. Streams, rivers, lakes, and the Atlantic Ocean provide swimming, fishing, surfing, and boating.

North Carolina has some of the best golfing in the nation. Many professional tournaments have been held in the state. In the mountains people can go to ski **resorts**. Also, there are many state parks where people can walk, hike, camp, and look at scenic North Carolina.

There are many professional and college sporting events for sports fans to watch. The Charlotte Motor Speedway is home to some of the most exciting car racing.

North Carolina also has indoor and outdoor theaters with excellent plays. There are festivals like the Highland games. Museums, battleground sites, and other historic sites make North Carolina a very fun state.

Girls dancing in the Highland Games, North Carolina.

North Carolina at Work

The people of North Carolina must work to make money. Early on, North Carolina was mostly a farming state. Today, the state has grown into a major **industrial** center. Most people work in **manufacturing**.

Workers at textile mills produce cotton, yarns, threads, and knitted goods. The people of North Carolina also manufacture clothing.

North Carolina is also the leader in **producing** cigarettes and other tobacco products. More than half of the nation's cigarettes are made here. Although smoking is a terrible habit and people should never start, making cigarettes has created thousands of jobs for the people of North Carolina for many years.

Workers in North Carolina make wood and paper products. Because of its many forests, North Carolina has always been near the top in lumbering.

There are more farms in North Carolina than any other Southeastern state. Farmers grow tobacco, corn, cotton, peanuts, oats, and fruits.

There are many different things to do in the Tar Heel State. Because of its beauty, weather, people, land, water, and mountains, North Carolina is a great place to visit, live, work, and play.

Lumbering is big business in North Carolina.

Fun Facts

- The highest point in North Carolina is Mount Mitchell. It is 6,684 feet (2,037 m) tall. The lowest area is where the ocean meets the land.
- North Carolina is the 29th biggest state. Its land covers 48,843 square miles (126,503 sq km). However, in **population,** it is the 10th largest state.
- When North Carolina was first being discovered, something very mysterious took place. In 1587, John White and a group of people settled on Roanoke Island. White went back to England for supplies and came back three years later. To his surprise, he found the island deserted. The people were never found, and today the "Lost Colony" is still a mystery.

• The first airplane to ever be flown took place over North Carolina. Two brothers, Orville and Wilbur Wright, took off near Kitty Hawk, North Carolina, and flew over the state. Kitty Hawk is a very historic site.

Wright Brothers Memorial, Kitty Hawk, North Carolina.

Glossary

American Revolution: a war that gave the United States its independence from Great Britain.
Border: neighboring states, countries, or waters.
Cattle: farm animals such as cows, bulls, and oxen.
Civil War: a war between groups within the same country.
Crops: what farmers grow on their farm to either eat or sell or do both.
Explorers: people who are some of the first to discover and look over land.
Hub: the center of action.
Industrial: big businesses such as factories or manufacturing.
Industry: many different types of businesses.
Manufacture: to make things by machine in a factory.
Native Americans: the first people who were born and lived in North America.
Population: the number of people living in a certain place.
Production: to make a lot of something.
Resort: a place to vacation that has fun things to do.
Rural: outside of the city.
Settlers: people that move to a new land where no one has lived before and build a community.
Tourists: people who travel for fun.

Internet Sites

North Carolina Encyclopedia
http://hal.dcr.state.nc.us/nc/cover.htm
This encyclopedia is designed to give you an overview of the people, the government, the history, and the resources of North Carolina. The information is organized into the broad information categories. Most of these categories offer an opportunity to select either more specific or additional information on a particular topic.

North Carolina Aquariums
http://www.aquariums.state.nc.us/Aquariums/
This website is not only fun and interactive, but it also promotes an awareness, understanding, appreciation, and conservation of the diverse natural and cultural resources associated with North Carolina's ocean, estuaries, rivers, streams, and other aquatic environments.

These sites are subject to change. Go to your favorite search engine and type in North Carolina for more sites.

PASS IT ON

Tell Others Something Special About Your State

To educate readers around the country, pass on interesting tips, places to see, history, and little unknown facts about the state you live in. We want to hear from you!
To get posted on ABDO & Daughters website, e-mail us at "mystate@abdopub.com"

Index

A
American Revolution 5
Atlantic Ocean 5, 8, 24

B
battlefields 5
British 4

C
cattle 5
Charlotte 6, 20, 24
cities 20, 21
Civil War 5, 11
Confederate soldiers 4
cotton 8, 26, 27
crops 8

E
Europeans 10
explorers 10

F
farms 4, 8, 23, 27
fishing 5, 24
forest 5, 8, 22, 23, 26

G
golf 24
Great Smoky Mountains 22

H
historic site 5, 25, 29

J
Jackson, Andrew 16, 18
Jordan, Michael 16, 18

K
King Charles I 12
Kitty Hawk 5, 16, 29

L
lakes 9, 22, 24
lumber 5, 26

M
Mount Mitchell 6, 22, 28
mountains 8, 22, 24, 27

N
Native Americans 10, 12, 18

P
parks 8, 9, 24
Polk, James K. 6, 16, 18
population 6, 20, 28

Q
Queen Elizabeth of England 12

R
Raleigh 6, 16, 18, 20
Raleigh, Sir Walter 10, 12
resorts 24
rivers 6, 9, 22, 23, 24
Roanoke Island 10, 12, 28

S
settlement 5

T
Tar Heel 4, 7, 9, 21, 27
Tar River 4
tourists 9

W
weather 8, 24, 27
Winston-Salem 21
Wright Brothers 5, 16

	DATE DUE		

3196039000485

975.6 Joseph, Paul.
JOS
North Carolina

LONGFELLOW ELEMENTARY LIBRARY
HOUSTON, TX. 77025

399629 01495   41694C   012